Dear (Potential) Friend,

Shalom,

S.V.W.

Love...Light...Life

To Be or Not to Be, a Mensch

Poems by Stuart V. Witt

Love ... Light ... Life

Copyright © 2024 by Stuart V. Witt

All rights reserved.

Published by Red Penguin Books

Bellerose Village, NY

ISBN

Digital 978-1-63777-548-6

Print 978-1-63777-549-3

No part of this book may be reproduced in any form or by any electronic or mechanical means, including information storage and retrieval systems, without written permission from the author, except for the use of brief quotations in a book review.

...Gratitude to my parents of blessed memory;

...Gratitude to kindred spirits everywhere.

With respect and with love to Civia and to Malka.

An Open Thank-You Letter

from Stuart V. Witt

to Stephanie Larkin

I had the chutzpah to ask you to turn my <u>manuscript</u> into a <u>work of art</u>. You did not recoil from my excessive request, but you, in the spirit of writer e.e. cummings, dressed each of my one plus seventy poems up. I ask (potential) readers to see how the poems appear for themselves.

Contents

Dear Reader	1
1. Beyond Our Puny Selves	2
2. Fault-finding No More	4
3. Modest Man	6
4. How to Get a Better Deal	8
5. Point and Counterpoint	10
6. Teach	12
7. Sadness and Joy	14
8. Joy	16
9. Eye Contact	18
10. Large and Little.	20
11. The Poet and The Poem	22
12. ...careless back and forth...	24
13. Sprouting Wings	26
14. Communion	28
15. Dire Consequences	30
16. Turn	32
17. Quite Backwards	34
18. Even There, Be Moderate	36
19. Forms of Beauty	38
20. Above? Below?	40
21. Choose One	42
22. Who am I?	44
23. Together, We Stand	46
24. Free Will	48
25. I Must Start Small	50
26. A Gulf Ever So Big	52
27. I Turn About	54
28. It's a long road from here...	56
29. One	58

30. My Will	60
31. Please Join In	62
32. Like a diamond, but not ...	64
33. The One in Charge	66
34. Umbrage	68
35. Let Go	70
36. Peck, Not	72
37. Human is not Divine	74
38. Seen or Unseen	76
39. Ilk of Guilt	78
40. Wondrous Offspring	80
41. Sad or Funny	82
42. What is really being asked?	84
43. A Better Choice	86
44. Renewal	88
45. Yes. Still more.	90
46. Get rid of greed...	92
47. We Cannot Keep Running	94
48. With Little or With Much	96
49. Reckoning	98
50. Panic Him Not	100
51. Opposite Reactions	102
52. Two Voices	104
53. I Hope You See	106
54. Social animals, aren't we?	108
55. Hypocrisy	110
56. Symbiosis	112
57. When We Sour...	114
58. Do much. Speak little.	116
59. Earnest Assessment	118
60. How can we manage better?	120
61. Be Not Too Narrow	122
62. Credit Due Woman	124
63. Sidestep Magic	126

64. Consider Corrections	128
65. Too Close to Sin	130
66. Good Humor, Seriously	132
67. Act responsibly...	134
68. Tough, but it need not be bleak...	136
69. Amidst the Muck	138
70. Love... Light... Life	140
71. Is brevity a mitzvah?	142
72. Like a Song	146
73. Gusto or Guffaw?	148
Additional Writings by Stuart V. Witt posted to Fan Story	150
Acknowledgments	155
About the Author	157

Dear Reader,

I hope you enjoy reading the poems in this book. Moreover, I hope that reading these poems will enhance the meaning, purpose, and beauty in your life. (Attempting the challenges might help. Also, reading poems out loud might help.) While I have this opportunity to address you personally, I hope that you will try to write three poems (or, if not poems, at least three "somethings") as your response to the following prompts:

1. Overcast

2. An Unexpected Opportunity

3. Yourself or Other People

1. Beyond Our Puny Selves

Some might feel the Deity's Presence

      within their own hearts and souls.

Some might bear witness to the Deity

      through cosmic wonders near or far.

Others might doubt (or even deny)

      that the Deity exists.

        If you doubt or if you deny,
        Try to find a substitute
        (For the Deity)
        That enlightens our lives.

Love...Light...Life

Challenge: Compare/contrast human to human with human to Deity interactions. Oh, what does the word "Deity" mean?

2. Fault-finding No More

Even if I am lowly, I am still a human being.

Anyone who casts aspersions upon me
Diminishes himself as he attempts to diminish me.

In my lowliness, I speak to my fellow human beings:
Seek out and nourish genuine glimmers of hope in me
And that might encourage you to do likewise in thee.

Challenge: If we mock others, does that help us? Why or why not?

3. Modest Man

He trumpets not himself.

He knows his inner worth.

        He nurtures his fellow human beings

        And thereby secures his rightful berth.

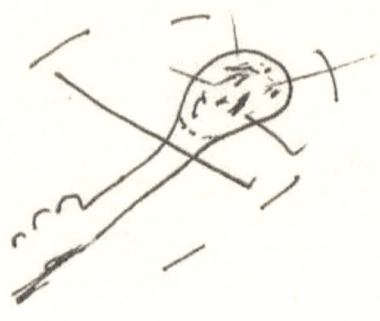

Love...Light...Life

Challenge: Why would a modest person nurture other people?

4. How to Get a Better Deal

If life appears to be passing us by,

    As waters passing between our fingers

        Or as shadows of persons we do not see,

If we are irked by mysteries all about us,

    Then we would be wise to recognize that

        We need to be lowly in order to evolve.

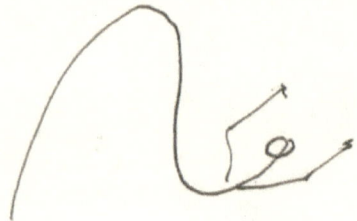

In antiquity, one person's lowliness

    Allowed him to see, within a log, a wheel.

        Our lowliness might teach us to be more real.

Challenge: How does arrogance hurt us?

5. Point and Counterpoint

To be buffeted about by ocean tides,
Physical or metaphysical,
Surely, that is part of our lives.

But why restrict ourselves there?

Why not be buoyed by spirits

Of wonder?

And of awe?

Challenge: How does seeing things from different perspectives help?

6. Teach

> I am your teacher.
> I am not Michelangelo.
> Michelangelo was a preeminent sculptor.
> He could bring out life, from stone.

Yes, I am your teacher.
No, you are not stone.
If you are willing to learn,
I will help you to do so.

Challenge: How are we dependent upon each other? What does that have to do with this poem?

7. Sadness and Joy

I felt mistreated.

Tears welled up from my eyes.

Released from my prison of sadness,

I now witness blue skies.

Challenge: Discuss how our feelings do or do not point us in a good direction.

8. Joy

Joy is an infant smiling,
   Seemingly well beyond its years.

Joy is a young child,
   Skipping without a fear.

Joy is a woman whose
   Smiles outperform her tears.

Joy is a man with boundaries.
   He does not stand 'nearer than near'.

Search for examples of your own,
   But do not grin ear to ear.

Challenge: Is joy unique to each person? Explore this.

9. Eye Contact

There was a lass and a lad,
Sister, brother, not yet ten, I think.

I am clearly an adult.

Our eyes happened to meet.

Our difference in years

Appeared to disappear.

In harmony, with each other, were we.

Challenge: *How can we overcome gender or age gaps?*

10. Large and Little.

Who plants sequoia trees?
Anyhow, it is many a year before
These
reach
their
majestic
heights.

Some plant tiny pansies.
We soon see them full size.
And pansies have tender smiles.

Love...Light...Life

Challenge: What, do you believe, is the essential message of this poem and why do you believe that?

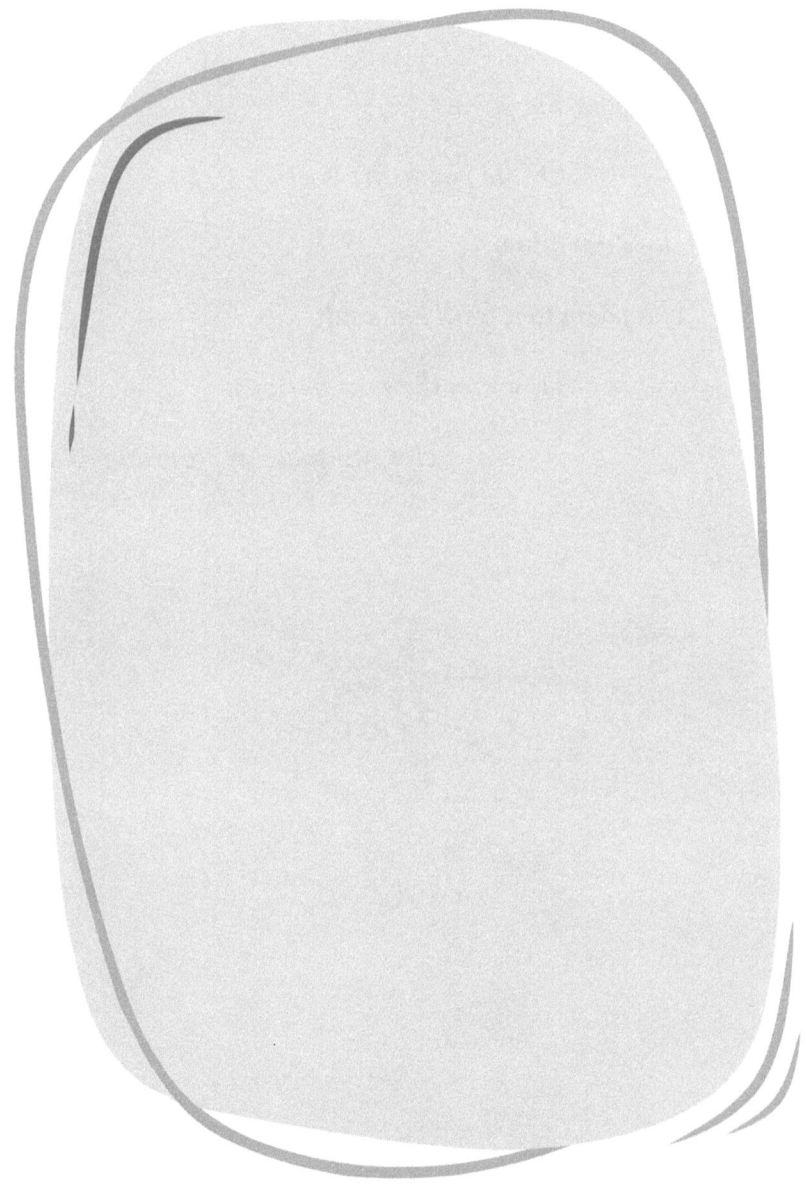

11. The Poet and The Poem

Who forms whom,

    The poet, the poem,

        Or the poem, the poet?

If the poet does not allow

    The poem to refresh her soul,

        How can the poet perform

            Her uniquely appropriate role?

Challenge: *Is there a tug of war between the poet and the poem? Just what is the relationship between the two? Discuss this.*

12. ...careless back and forth...

If you harm me

                                      And I, in turn, harm you

And if, in our tit for tat,

                    We something like a landslide cause,

A nightmare far beyond us two,

                              Then how will we react to

                Our
                    knee-jerk
                          tragic
                                  fall?

Challenge: How do narrow-mindedness or broad-mindedness influence outcomes in our lives? Discuss this carefully.

13. Sprouting Wings

If I man up for my faults,

    Then as a caterpillar becomes

        A butterfly or a moth,

              too.

          myself

       uplift

    might

I

Challenge: Can admitting our weaknesses transform our lives for the better? Explore this idea with as much openness as you can muster.

14. Communion

Pure joy pours forth

From her infant sister

As this young girl

Sounds out words,

Silently, before her.

Challenge: *What is communion and how can we nurture communion in our lives?*

15. Dire Consequences

If my fears

                                        (Or my covetousness)

Wall me off from

The tortured,

                                        The dispossessed,

Or the abandoned,

                Woe unto me
                If the earth
              Swallows me up
            As it did to Korah
          And to his followers.

Challenge: If we do not care about the suffering of others, is that likely to have a bad effect on ourselves? Why do you think that? (Give supporting arguments.)

16. Turn

Is the goal of American Football
To turn boys into men?

What if the rules are turned,
To avoid life diminishing injury?

Can this sport handle such a turn?

Can the boys?

Can the men?

Challenge: How can we determine which risks are reasonable?

17. Quite Backwards

Jump from a mountain peak?

Call on the Deity to rescue us?

Is the Deity our servant?

Are we mortals, His masters?

Challenge: If we act as though we do not care about our lives, does that encourage the Deity to be supportive towards us?

18. Even There, Be Moderate

Yes, honor our fellows,

But do avoid hyperbole,

Lest our fellows become swell-headed

And (even by loved ones) dreaded.

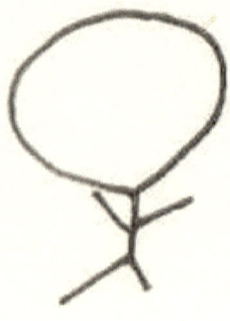

Challenge: Do we function better, if we think more of ourselves than we merit? Support your response. Oh, what does the word "hyperbole" mean?

19. Forms of Beauty

Flowers with splendid colors.

Children who rejoice in their siblings.

Challenge: Try to discover different kinds of beauty. If you are successful, try to explore them.

20. Above? Below?

```
                        Heaven.
                towards
            reaches
        plant
      this
    of
  stem
The
That
   flower's
       petals
         bow
            towards
                Earth.
```

Nobility... Humility... Upon our mortal journey.

Challenge: Try to apply the words "Nobility" and "Humility" in your life and/or in the lives of other people.

21. Choose One

A humble truthful person.

A person devoted to magic.

Who is more reliable?

Who is more desirable?

Challenge: Explore the above personality types in yourself and/or in other people.

22. Who am I?

Glimpsing a dawn of self-awareness,

I see myself as pendulum,

Here grandiose,   there depressive.

But I wish to be more metronome than pendulum,

Little by little, to harmonize with reality.

Challenge: "And this too shall pass" is supposed to apply in difficult and in easy times. How does the quoted statement relate to this poem?

23. Together, We Stand

When someone builds bridging gifts,

Through caring words,

Through heartfelt smiles,

Or through wordless songs,

Let us relinquish each petty thought.

Let us shun a grudge.

Love...Light...Life

Challenge: Is it important to show gratitude for what is good in our lives? Why?

24. Free Will

If an evil thought tempts me to be crass,
I can affirm my better self,
At least for now.

                If a thought, noble and refined, enters my mind,
                              I can be inspired by it,
                                    At least for now.

        The choice is, at least partly, mine.

Challenge: Is free will absolute or conditional? Justify your answer.

25. I Must Start Small

If I would only master some simple skills:

"Hello."
"You have a lovely smile."
"Let us help each other with that."
"What can I learn from what you did?"

Cutthroat competing receding,

                        Friends we might become.

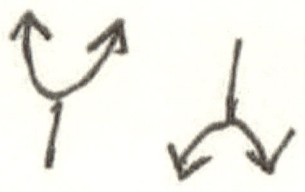

Love...Light...Life

Challenge: Is it important to start small and to build from there? Why?

26. A Gulf Ever So Big

If there should arise a rift
between yourself　　　　　　　　and one you love
And your attempts to harmonize are rebuffed,
Step back　　　　　　from the abyss.

Greet every wallflower with good cheer.
Smile with gratitude at every daffodil
That crosses your path.
Become a master rift mender.
Serve others well.
As for your wounds,
Be compassionate towards yourself.

If the Deity is so inclined...

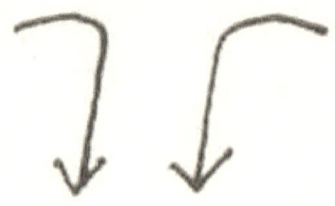

Challenge: How can we adjust and adapt to life's disappointments?

27. I Turn About

If, when impoverished,

I share with others

What little I have,

        My misfortune,

        I rout.

Love...Light...Life

Challenge: How can we overcome our misfortune by sharing what little we have?

28. It's a long road from here . . .

      Am I attuned to the Deity?

    To Heaven and to Earth?

To minerals, plants, animals, and humankind?

My character is not that august.

    From here, move forward, I must.

Love...Light...Life

Challenge: Give examples of how we mortals are limited in our lives. What can we accomplish with, but not without, the Deity's help?

29. One

> *Buddhists ask,*
> *"What is the sound of one hand clapping?"*

Let me try my hand at this,

Not as a Buddhist, but as a Jew.

> *Suppose the Deity speaks to me in a vision*
> *And asks me to clap hands with Him.*
> *The idea is to get the attention of humankind*
> *So that the Deity might speak with them.*
> *But suppose, awestruck by this vision,*
> *I do not clap hands with the Deity.*

"What is the sound of one hand clapping?"

Now, I hope, you can answer as well as I can.

Challenge: Is life an ongoing process? How do you know?

30. My Will

I was a good beginning skier,

With good beginning skills,

But my confidence was amiss

And a tree that was

Planted firmly in the earth

Charged menacingly at me.

        I executed a turn

        And now, still alive,

        I recite this poem to you.

Challenge: Give examples of how it is important to exercise our will.

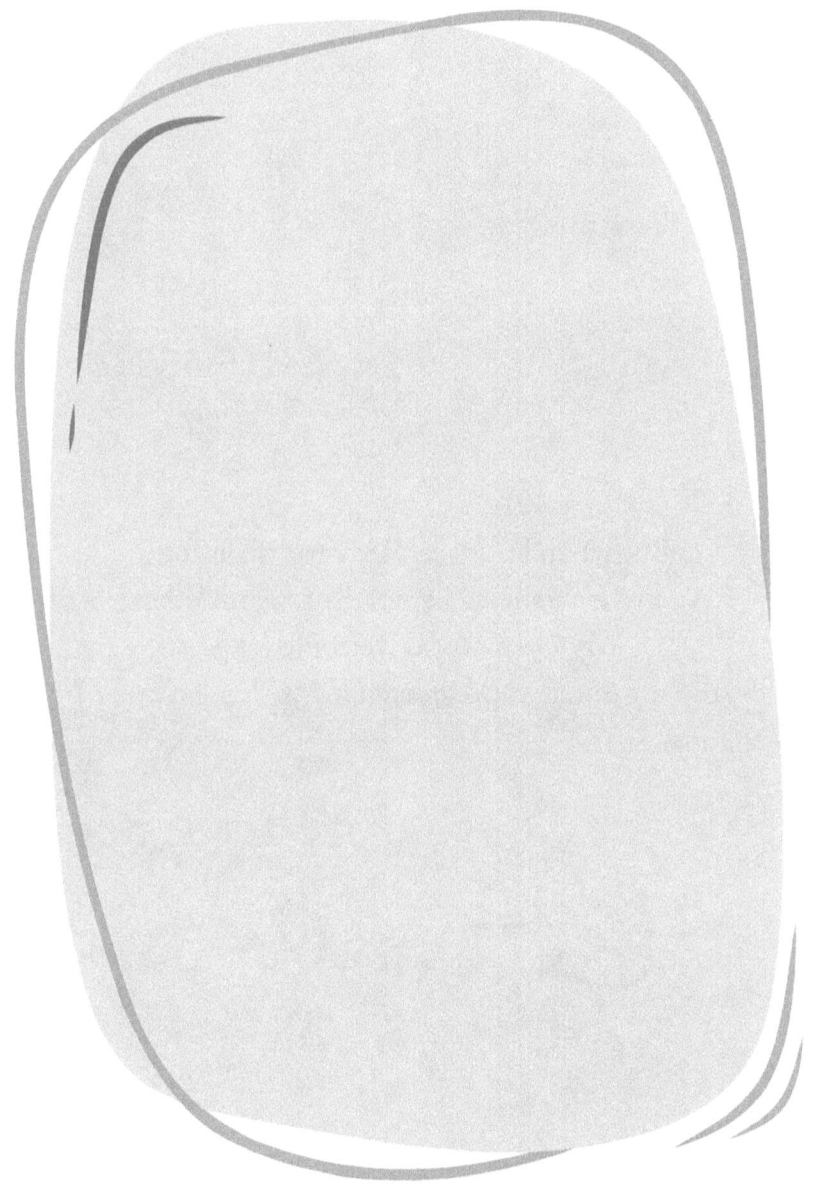

31. Please Join In

Not that long ago,

    I walked outdoors.

        Snow snowed.

            Wind gusted.

                I was (and I felt) pelted.

But when I transcended my discomfort
And when I showed empathy towards others,
My inner world welcomed me.
And my outer world greeted me with open arms.

Love...Light...Life

Challenge: Does self-pity help? Why or why not?

32. Like a diamond, but not ...

A diamond is a unique kind of rock
        And no two diamonds are alike.

Humans become more unique as
        Vessels for Divine Light and Life.

Reflexively, dispute me not.
        First try it. Then see if I am right.

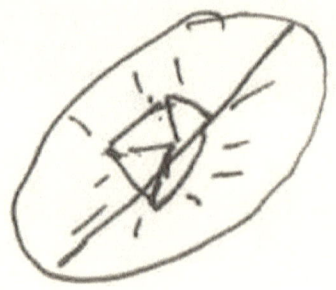

Challenge: How can we all become more unique by being receptive to Divine Light and Life?

33. The One in Charge

That which I desire most,

My master has become.

                    I am as I was before,

                        But in servitude as well.

          Master my desires?

      Let my desires master myself?

Challenge: Is blindly following our desires good or bad? Justify your answer.

34. Umbrage

I said, "Your offense is unforgivable."

        But if I see only recent blows,
        Not blows linking back to antiquity
        And if my subsequent wrath is toxic,

                Whose offense is unforgivable?

Challenge: Does mercy apply only to ourselves or to others too? Why?

35. Let Go

Let that delicate bird fly free...

                        Or butterfly...

                Or child whose spirits soar...

        Or elder with wisdom to impart...

Open your heart, soul, and fist

                        And with wonder

                Let those free spirits depart

(And return, if or when these do wish.)

***Challenge:** Is it good to be possessive or controlling of others? Discuss this matter.*

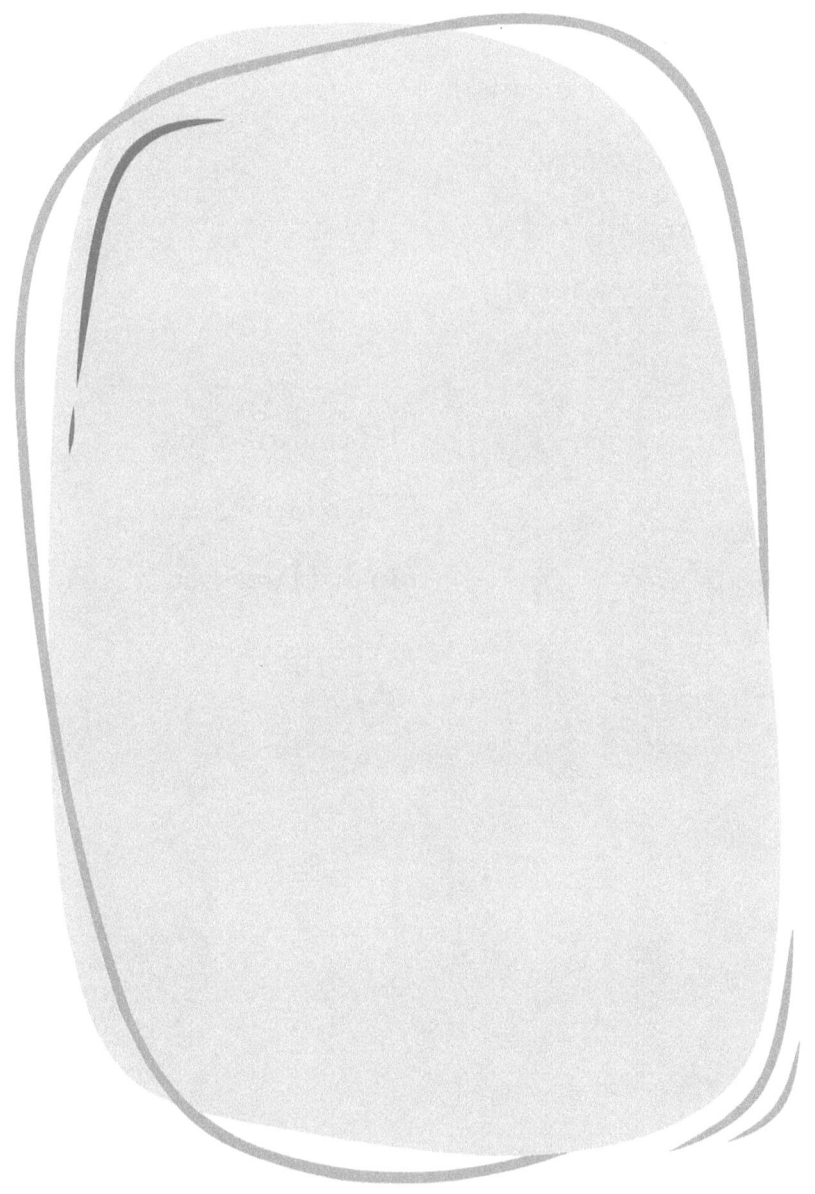

36. Peck, Not

If I am right and I know it

And if you are wrong,

But in error,

you 'know' you are right,

                              If I embarrass you,

                              Then I wrong you,

                              In that I treat you

                              With disrespect.

Challenge: Do the ignorant not deserve disrespect? Why or why not?

37. Human is not Divine

Cast into a trance,

        By authority or by charm,

Of physician or of 'lance',

        Arise. Forestall grievous harm.

Love...Light...Life

Challenge: Can authority or charm be misleading? How?

38. Seen or Unseen

Within a beggar woman,

See no hint of a queen?

        Within a queen,

        See no hint of a beggar woman?

    Glean.

Love...Light...Life

Challenge: How is this poem similar to and also different from the poem immediately before it?

39. Ilk of Guilt

    If a woman were to weep, smile, or laugh,

If she were to reveal her feelings to me,

    If she were to fall upon her knees,

If I callously turn my back,

    How am I human,

Except in a promise unfulfilled?

Challenge: Are gender differences important? Would this poem also apply to a man?

40. Wondrous Offspring

Told, "Fulfill these urgent tasks",

        If I respond, "These are a burden to me",

Let my feelings be birthing pangs.

        Let me give birth to Empathy, to Compassion.

Challenge: This might appear obvious, but why are self-absorption and speaking down to people bad things?

41. Sad or Funny

Upon a spider web, within a palace,

Someone carelessly

                steps.

The spider shouts:

"Run. The palace is f

                a

                l

                l

              ing."

Challenge: What misleading assumption overcomes the spider? Are we humans subject to that error? Give an example, if "yes". If "no". Why not?

42. What is really being asked?

A question is as embryo

Within its mother's womb.

Pause.

Decipher the need.

　　　　　　　　　　　Only then, respond.

Challenge: Just how is a question like an embryo?

43. A Better Choice

In hot pursuit of glory,

Is there room for anything else?

Instead, we could eat manna from Heaven.

And we could drink well water

                        from

                              Earth.

Love...Light...Life

Challenge: Does the search for glory enhance or diminish us? Carefully discuss this.

44. Renewal

I forgive you.

That gives both of us a fresh start.

Is that not part of life's art?

Challenge: Discuss the poem in your own words. What is the poem's meaning? Is forgiveness good or bad? How so?

45. Yes. Still more.

We have been told:
Water these plants;
Walk the dog.

                                    For fellow human beings:
                                        Walk in their shoes;
                                        Speak to their hearts.

Love...Light...Life

Challenge: Is this one poem or two poems? Is there a unified theme? What is the connection between the two stanzas, if any?

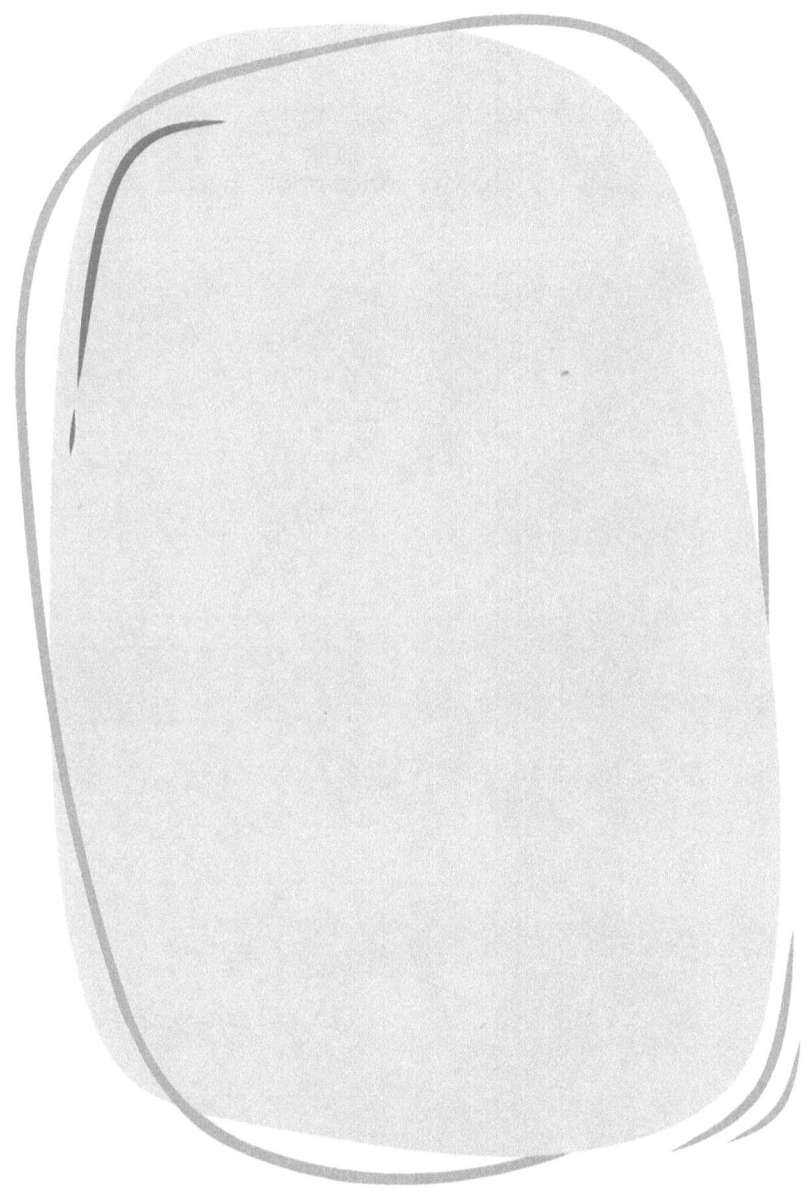

46. Get rid of greed...

Loving kindness is as a gentle breeze

    That refreshes our hearts and

        That responds to our needs.

Challenge: Is loving kindness really that healing? How so?

47. We Cannot Keep Running

Eve was won over by
The serpent's cunning.

Life was no longer stunning.

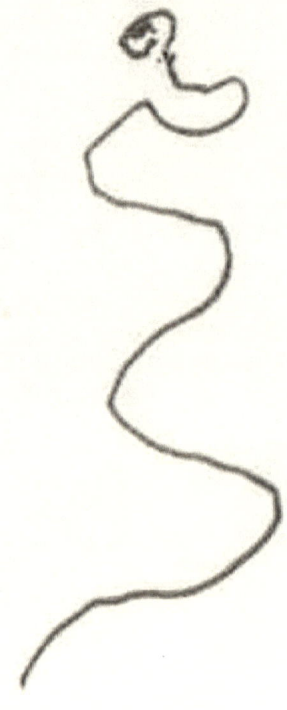

Challenge: What does the word "naïve" mean? How can we avoid being naïve?

48. With Little or With Much

Do our footprints match our blessings?

Life requires bending,

        tending,

            mending...

Challenge: Is it right to expect more from us if we have a head start in life? Tell us more about that.

49. Reckoning

                Alone, Joseph wept.

Not yet time
To weep upon
His brothers' necks.

                                      When his brothers
                                      Showed genuine remorse,
                                      That time would beckon.

Challenge: Is it possible to forgive a person (or several people) too early? Why do you think your answer is right?

50. Panic Him Not

If, with rambunctious man,

    We are calm and collected,

If we do not intrude,

    But treat him respectfully,

If, when he approaches,

    We, ourselves, act appropriately,

Though lightning strike,

    Perhaps no harm will be inflicted.

Love...Light...Life

Challenge: Does the expression "better safe than sorry" apply to this poem? And what does "rambunctious" mean?

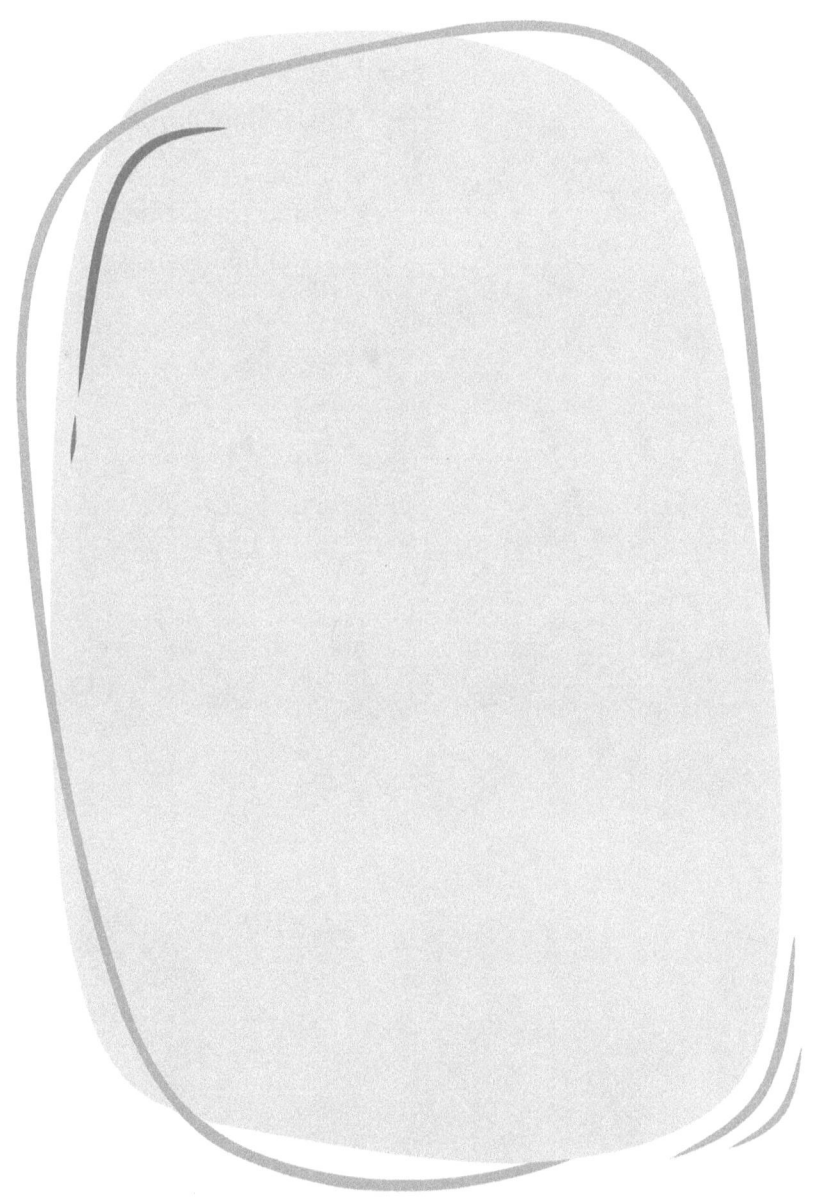

51. Opposite Reactions

> Shall we rejoice in the strides of
> Our fellow human beings?
>
> Or shall we deride them for
> Their transgressions?

Challenge: Which of the two approaches described in this poem is more likely to bring out the best in people? Why so?

52. Two Voices

                                  Your attractive side turns the tide
                                            In inspiring directions.

Yet we clash.
Why the volcanic eruptions?

Challenge: Discuss how in some manners we might be progressing well, as human beings, whereas in other manners we might be sorely lacking.

53. I Hope You See

If I nurture myself,

Especially when I am turned off by me,

I do not play second fiddle to a tree.

Challenge: Might a tree need nurturing? Might we? Are there special moments when we need more nurturing than in other moments? Please discuss these matters.

54. Social animals, aren't we?

In a boa constrictor's grip,

                                      Be not stoically alone,

But give (and receive) help.

Challenge: Are we social animals? Potentially? Does it require a boa constrictor for us to conduct ourselves in a socially appropriate manner? Explore these ideas.

55. Hypocrisy

If my speech is noble and refined,
But my deeds forswear virtue,

My head and heart are not aligned,
Or my will is dormant.

Challenge: Is a positive self-image important? What if we do not live up to a positive self-image? What is next? Discuss...Oh, what does the word "forswear" mean?

56. Symbiosis

The bees fertilize the flowers.

Bees and flowers are empowered.

Challenge: Try to see if symbiosis applies to human beings, especially to human beings with substantially different personalities or characters. Share your thoughts on this.

57. When We Sour…

Shower?

Vaunt our power?

Become dour?

Challenge: If we slide down a slippery slope, how can we redirect ourselves for our benefit and for the benefit of other people?

58. Do much. Speak little.

If our belief in the Deity rings hollow,

Let us nurture our fellow human beings.

                                          Let us reach out to the troubled.

Challenge: Can our attempts at piety miss the mark? By far? How can we correct the course? Give an example and try to be as specific as you can be.

59. Earnest Assessment

If, as this plant, I am vibrant

And if, with my environment,

I am in harmony,

Let me sojourn further.

                                         If not, let me journey onward.

Love...Light...Life

Challenge: Is it good to be a vibrant human being? And to be in harmony with our environment? What do you think of the conclusions of this poem? Discuss these matters carefully.

60. How can we manage better?

Shall we perish out of sadness?

        Shall we murder out of anger?

                Let us cherish cosmic wonders.

Let us mentor others.

Challenge: Is it good to allow our emotions to control our thinking, our speech, or our actions? Respond to this question in as specific a manner as you can.

61. Be Not Too Narrow

Worship our money?

                        Thrust our power like daggers?

Show kindness to others?

Challenge: Do we have the power to improve the world, at least a tiny bit? Is it worth the effort? Why or why not?

62. Credit Due Woman

        Man or woman can birth a poem.

Only woman can birth a child.

        Embryo grows within her womb.

At miracle's end, comes forth the child.

        She nurses the child with her good milk,

But her heart's goodness is surpassing.

Challenge: Are there specific good tendencies that are more likely to characterize women? What can men best learn from women? How can men and women work better, together?

63. Sidestep Magic

Become wise without effort?

Is a diamond formed without pressure?

Not distinguish between folly and wisdom?

Does a good gardener neglect pruning?

Challenge: Look up the meaning of "magical thinking". Is "magical thinking" a key element in this poem? Why do you think so?

64. Consider Corrections

Whirlpools of willfulness.

Seas of self-absorption.

Tsunamis of tyranny.

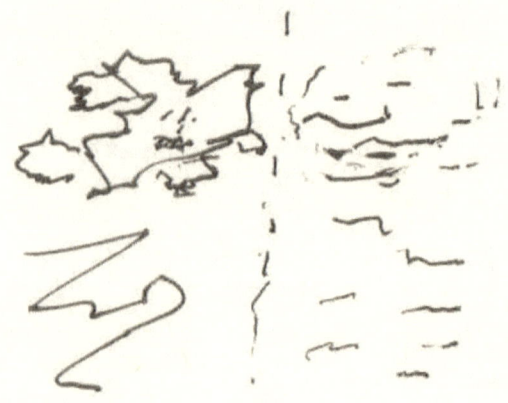

Tranquility?

Love...Light...Life

Challenge: Is this poem coherent? Does it form a unified whole? Show us how you arrived at your conclusions.

65. Too Close to Sin

Laugh to fit in?
Or to accompany a fiendish grin?

Challenge: If receiving approval has huge importance to us, are we more vulnerable to sin? Share your thinking on that.

66. Good Humor, Seriously

Laughter is an uplifting companion
If we learn to gently chuckle
At our own foibles.

Challenge: Describe this poem in your own words. Can laughter lead us to more insight about ourselves? How so?

67. Act responsibly...

In uncertain times,
In unchartered waters,
Let cool heads arise above us.
At night, let moon and stars guide us.

We need to avoid shallow shoals.

We need to steer clear of cunning seas.

Let us disavow extremes.

Let us rejoice in the moderate.

Challenge: In threatening circumstances, what kinds of precautions might be helpful? Why do you think that?

68. Tough, but it need not be bleak…

Thronged by wrong, cleave to right.
Companions, like-minded, seek.

Try hard not to be a geek.

Love...Light...Life

Challenge: If people, where they live, for example, are surrounded by evil practices, how can these people avoid being sucked into the evil which surrounds them?

69. Amidst the Muck

Life is unfair, as though a tsunami struck,

        Or, in fact, it did.

Let us assume we are still alive.

Others fare better (or worse) than ourselves.

        Some cannot see beyond themselves.

Some can and do.

        Shall we resort to primal screams?

      Shall we call upon the Supreme Being?

    Shall we nurture each other?

Challenge: Are the suggestions mutually exclusive? Why?

70. Love... Light... Life

Held close, we hear and we feel
The reassuring beats of our mothers' hearts.

        With time, mother and father become the Deity,
                Our new/old Source of Life.

    Then, it falls upon us to reassure others,
    For to the Deity, our own heartbeats belong.

Challenge: Is this poem sensible? Why or why not?

71. Is brevity a mitzvah?

1. Grist for Our Mills

> Life is not all bliss.
> At times, we miss.

2. Too Much Zest

> Run from the devil,
> But fall into his ditch?

3. Not Just a Blip

> Lies grip our lips;
> We tend to trip.

Challenge: Discuss the above three poems in terms of the question, "Is brevity a mitzvah?"

Love...Light...Life

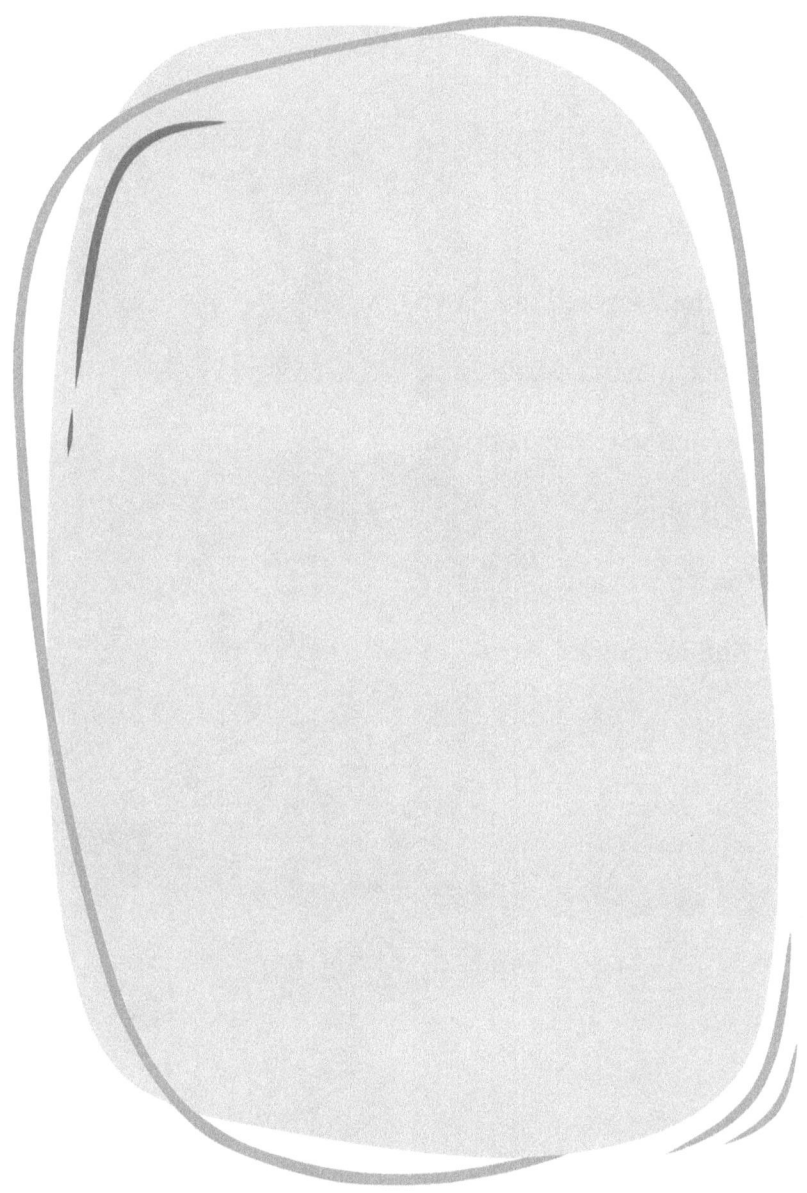

72. Like a Song

A woman shouted.

A man walked off.

Then, others walked or talked.

After that, a man addressed

The woman who had shouted:

"What is wrong?"

The two conversed.

The woman calmed.

Love...Light...Life

Challenge: Poem? Story? Both? Neither?

Why do you think so? Further comments?

73. Gusto or Guffaw?

Alive

Show drive.

Do not connive.

In a beehive?

Foolish dive?

Work to thrive.

Have you arrived?

Love...Light...Life

Challenge: Gusto or Guffaw? And please try to justify which of those two words apply to this poem.

Additional Writings by Stuart V. Witt posted to Fan Story

Prompt #1:

Write a story that is between 100 and 150 words. You must use the words "art", "final", "beauty", "sudden", coward".

My response to prompt #1:

Assert yourself...

Do not be stubborn, Shirley.

Herman, you are a coward.

How so, Shirley?

Love...Light...Life

Any sudden move, you flinch.

I just do not like sudden moves.

You are stubborn, Herman.

I am stubborn? I am a coward?

Yes, Herman.

Shirley, do I have a good quality?

Not really, Herman.

Do you want a divorce, Shirley?

No. I do not believe in divorces.

Keep married for that alone?

Yes, Herman.

We need to do better, Shirley.

No, Herman. That is my final word.

Shirley, marriage is an art.

Herman, there is no beauty for us.

Let us visit something that has beauty.

Why Herman?

Because it is important to me, Shirley.

Oh? Really?

Prompt #2:

Write a one-minute comedic play, using at least two speaking characters. Do not exceed 200 words, including stage directions.

My response to Prompt #2:

Truthfully!

Jim: Stop writing truths.

Jessica: Why?

Jim: It puts us in a bad light.

Jessica: I need to spotlight badness.

Jim: Do you want people to mock us?

Jessica: We need to laugh at ourselves.

Jim: We look foolish.

Jessica: Do not be foolish.

Jim: We are foolish.

Jessica: Now, you are truthful.

Jim: Is that good?

Jessica: It is better than lies.

Acknowledgments

To Rabbi Kass: Rabbi Alvin Kass was my congregational rabbi for many years, and if there is any wisdom contained in this book, I believe that Rabbi Alvin Kass deserves credit.

To Barbara Novack: I gained writing skills under Barbara Novack's leadership in her Creative Writing Workshops, and I thank her. For any deficiencies in my writing, I accept full responsibility.

I thank Michael Lenderman for his very special support, technical and otherwise.

Manuscript to Book,
She never me Forsook,
Thank you, Stephanie Larkin

Appreciatively,
    Stuart V. Witt

About the Author

Stuart V. Witt taught High School Mathematics for numerous years. Now he writes poems (and sometimes short stories). He hopes to merge his interests in communicating through poems and in communicating through mathematics. If he succeeds, he will not be the first one to accomplish that. But he tries to build an integrated personality out of all his activities (exercise, poems, mathematics, socializing, etc.).

I include my photograph here <u>not</u> because my photograph is so great but as another means of communicating with any readers that I might be fortunate enough to have. I apologize to readers for not including their photographs, as well, but I hope that will not be feasible. Besides, readers have other means of participating such as responding to challenges or by using this book as a focus for discussion groups, at work or at play.

Readers, you have my very best wishes for proactive rewarding reading (and rereading). Go from strength to strength.

www.ingramcontent.com/pod-product-compliance
Lightning Source LLC
Chambersburg PA
CBHW030553080526
44585CB00012B/361